This book belongs to

Anastacia

(witch in training)

Spells for a perfect love life

Lauren White

**Andrews McMeel
Publishing**

Kansas City

♡ CONTENTS ♡

frog / prince!

chapter

How to use this book

How to use this book

Racing pulse, aching heart, bashful lover, wandering eyes, jaded love-life, lovers' tiff?... You need Magic; it's the cure-all for every romantic dilemma. To enhance YOUR love-life, read on...

A note about ingredients...

Love spells always call for the very best ingredients. Buy the most expensive, gorgeous, delicious things that you can possibly afford...

Look up your chosen spell well
in advance so that you can
gather the appropriate ingredients...

Plan where and when you are
going to perform your spell and
simply follow the instructions...

"A...B...C"

The right atmosphere is vital. Take as much time as you need and ensure that the space feels completely comfortable.

A spell performed with good motives and love in your heart will have the greatest effect. Remember, love really does make the world go 'round.

♡ THE SPELLS ♡

A brief description at the start of each spell will tell you, at a glance, its uses and applications...

There is also a key that gives a guide to the difficulty, reliability, and timing of each spell...

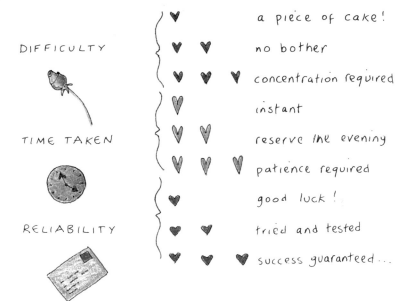

DIFFICULTY

♥ — a piece of cake!

♥ ♥ — no bother

♥ ♥ ♥ — concentration required

TIME TAKEN

♥ — instant

♥ ♥ — reserve the evening

♥ ♥ ♥ — patience required

RELIABILITY

♥ — good luck!

♥ ♥ — tried and tested

♥ ♥ ♥ — success guaranteed...

As with all things "practice makes perfect." As your confidence grows, you can adapt or personalize some spells, or perhaps devise your own...

secret "vial"

c h a p t e r

Making a love chest

How to make a love chest

This is the beginning of a long journey through a lifetime of love and romance. To begin you must prepare.

Over the years you will gather many significant and magical artifacts that you will want to treasure. So you will need somewhere special to keep them.

Your box must be special to you ～
Scour flea markets and antiques fairs or
make your own.

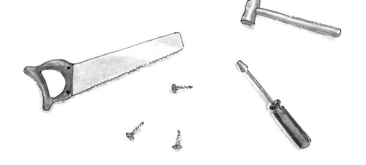

As long as it's at least the size of
a shoe box and you love it, it will
be a perfect place to store your
treasures.

Preparing your box

Mix together a confetti of:

- ♡ rose petals
- ♡ dried lavender
- ♡ jasmine flowers

Add a pinch of dried orrisroot to "fix" the fragrance and sprinkle with rose absolute essential oil.

Strew the mixture inside your special chest. You may also like to store a photograph of yourself, along with this little book in your box.

This is the beginning of your journey.

"the web"

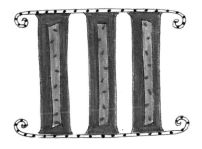

Get ready for love

GOLDEN FUTURE

This spell represents your "evergreen" and enduring faith in yourself and your quest for true love. Gold will never tarnish or fade and nor will your dreams for a golden future...

DIFFICULTY	TIME TAKEN	RELIABILITY
♥ ♥	♥ ♥	♥ ♥ ♥

☆ gold leaf

☆ This is available from good art and craft shops - (Read the instructions first).

two fresh evergreen leaves

photograph of yourself

find or make a small frame for your photograph

METHOD

(i) By the light of the full moon, lay out your tools and materials.

(ii) Carefully press your thumb on each leaf to leave an invisible imprint.

(iii) Gently press the gold leaf over the place where you put your thumb print. It will adhere to the surface of the leaf.

This will leave your energy encased in gold.

(iv) Place one leaf behind your photograph in the frame.

(v) Choose your moment and cast the other leaf to the four winds. (A moving car can make this very liberating!)

You now have one "imprint" grounded, nurtured and the other making its way in the world. These two sides of the self will always protect each other.

ACCENTUATE THE POSITIVE!

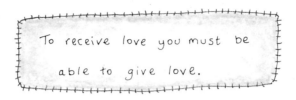

To receive love you must be able to give love.

This is a simple spell to celebrate YOU and all the positive qualities you have to share with someone special. As your awareness of them grows, so will other people's.

glowing with positive energy!!!

DIFFICULTY	TIME TAKEN	RELIABILITY
♥ ♥	♥ ♥ ♥	♥ ♥ ♥

♡ YOU WILL NEED ♡

fine quality
notepaper and
pen

ribbon

(favorite
color)

lock of your hair

candle

 **METHOD**

(i) Tear up the paper into fourteen small squares.

(ii) On the evening of a new moon, light the candle and think of something good about yourself. Write it down on one of the squares of paper.

(iii) On another square of paper, write down something that you don't like about yourself and burn it in the candle flame.

(iv) Repeat steps (ii) and (iii) every night for one week.

(v) Tuck a lock of hair among the seven remaining squares of paper and bind the whole lot together with the ribbon.

All of your positive attributes will shine out for everyone to see, while your not-so-good points will disperse along with the smoke from the candle.

⭐ You might like to keep the bundle in your love chest ~ for luck ~

DON'T JUST SIT THERE!

Throw away that chocolate bar, turn off the television, and perform this spell. In no time at all there will be an army of suitors knocking on your door!

DIFFICULTY	TIME TAKEN	RELIABILITY
♥	♥	♥ ♥

♡ YOU WILL NEED ♡

chilled white wine

1tsp. cinnamon powder

pinch of sugar

METHOD (i) Fill the glass with wine,
sugar, and a tiny pinch of cinnamon.

(ii) Sprinkle the remaining cinnamon across
your threshold.

This simple offering will inspire the "right"
person to call on you before long.

STAR ATTRACTION

There is a way to get people to sit up and take notice! This spell is so simple and effective you will get immediate results – promise!

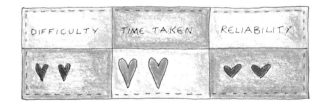

DIFFICULTY	TIME TAKEN	RELIABILITY
♥ ♥	♥ ♥	♥ ♥

✫ This is especially useful if there is a particular person in mind who simply "hasn't seen the light!"

♡ YOU WILL NEED ♡

four white candles

small mirror

(powder compact is perfect!)

a starlit night

 METHOD (i) Light the candles.

(ii) Carefully place them on the floor to form a square ∼ about two feet apart.

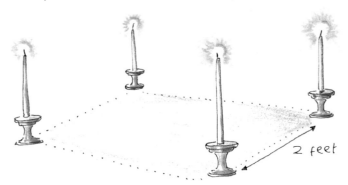

2 feet

(iii) Stand, surrounded by the candles, and hold the mirror up to "catch" the starlight while you say the words:

star shine
star light
make my aura
twice as bright

⭐ VERY IMPORTANT ~ Now cover the mirror.

When you want to
"shine," take out the
mirror and look into it.
The "captured" energy
will be reflected in
your eyes.

love potion

chapter

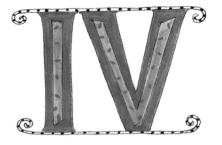

New romantics!

BEES AROUND THE HONEY POT

If you've got your eye on someone in particular, but they need a nudge in the right direction, this is the spell for you!

DIFFICULTY	TIME TAKEN	RELIABILITY
♥ ♥	♥	♥ ♥

This spell is performed in two stages ~

THE POTION

♡ YOU WILL NEED ♡

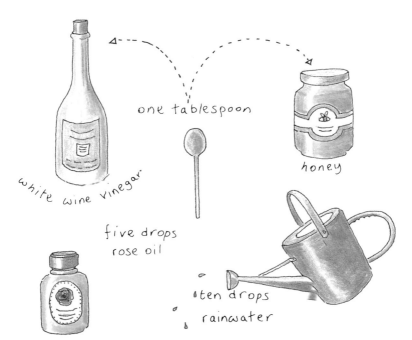

one tablespoon

white wine vinegar

honey

five drops
rose oil

ten drops
rainwater

METHOD

By the light of a new moon...
Mix all of the ingredients
together thoroughly.

THE SPELL

YOU WILL NEED

small bottle

pink ribbon

sealing wax and matches

METHOD

(i) Pour the potion into the tiny bottle and seal with wax.

(ii) Tie the ribbon around the bottle neck so that it can hang like a pendant.

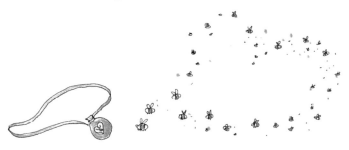

Wear it, secretly hung around your neck beneath your clothing, and listen for the sound of buzzing.

"I.D"

This is a quickie spell if you want to
know the identity of an admirer.

DIFFICULTY	TIME TAKEN	RELIABILITY
♥	♥	♥

YOU WILL NEED

apple

knife

white candle

This spell must be performed outside on a quiet night

(i) Burn a white candle for purity and honesty.

(ii) Carefully peel the apple so that the skin remains in one long strip.

(iii) Close your eyes and throw the peel over your left shoulder.

(iv) Turn to see the initial of your admirer's first name revealed by the shape of the peel.

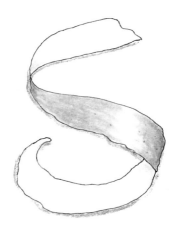

Eat the apple and save the seeds. They will form a magical souvenir when you and your love are finally united.

A CURE FOR SHYNESS

Sometimes a shy or reticent lover may need gently "reeling in."

In this spell it is done with a silken cord! (If you haven't got one on hand, rope or heavy ribbon will suffice.)

DIFFICULTY	TIME TAKEN	RELIABILITY
♥	♥	♥ ♥

A handful each of ～

- ♡ laurel leaves . . . . . for bruvery
- ♡ marigolds . . . . for love
- ♡ lavender . . . . for purity and protection
- ♡ peppercorns . . . . . for heat and passion

METHOD (i) Arrange the rope or ribbon so that it forms a wide circle and scatter the dry ingredients inside the circle.

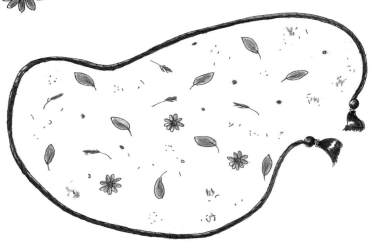

(ii) Step inside the circle.

(iii) Close your eyes.

(iv) Call your loved one to come to you.

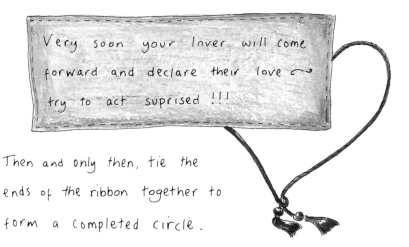

Very soon your lover will come
forward and declare their love ⌒
try to act suprised !!!

Then and only then, tie the
ends of the ribbon together to
form a completed circle.

"eternal flame"

chapter

True love

LOVE BOMB!

This is a spell for "pepping up" a faltering relationship. It's a risky one because it usually means "make or break" but sometimes you need to know if you're dealing with a firecracker or a damp squib!

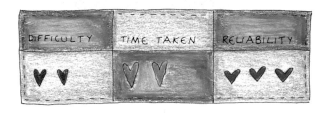

DIFFICULTY	TIME TAKEN	RELIABILITY
♥ ♥	♥ ♥	♥ ♥ ♥

YOU WILL NEED

A pinch of :

white pepper

lemongrass

(to focus the mind)

dried basil

a tiny piece of your fingernail

tiny red heart ~
(cut out of fabric or paper...)

lidded container

silver foil

☆ see note

☆ NOTE The original manuscript called
for a small bag made from the "hide
of a white rabbit". Silver foil is much
less stomach-churning AND
kinder to rabbits!

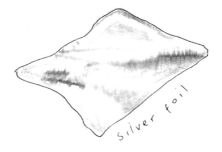

METHOD

(i) Place the pepper, basil, finger nail, and lemon grass into the container, replace the lid, and shake vigorously for at least two minutes.

(This is a powerful mixture - handle carefully.)

(ii) Sprinkle on the foil along with the heart and wrap up to make a tiny package.

This little parcel can then be subtly slipped into, say, a briefcase or sockdrawer. If your lover has serious intentions they will experience an "explosion" of love and desire, so prepare for a dynamite love affair!

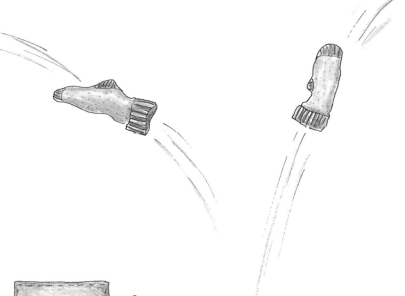

NOTE OF CAUTION

Only use this spell if you're prepared for the consequences because it has the power to blow your socks off !!!

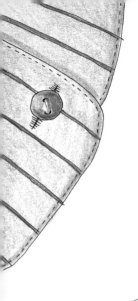

ON THE BUTTON

If you suspect that your loved one's thoughts are not entirely focused on you — and you alone: perform this spell.

DIFFICULTY	TIME TAKEN	RELIABILITY
♥	♥	♥ ♥

♡ YOU WILL NEED ♡

a garment belonging to your lover ~ such as a jacket

rose pink thread

small mother · of · pearl button

strand of your hair

red candles - one for each letter of your name

METHOD

(i) light the candles forming a ring around the button.

(ii) Take the needle and pass it through each flame in turn whispering the letter of your name it represents.

"A"

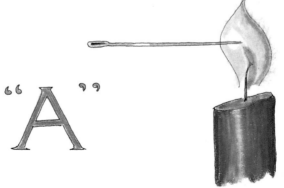

(iii) Twist the hair and thread together and use to sew the button to a secret place inside the jacket using the prepared needle.

✷ Just inside a pocket or the lining of a sleeve are good places.

(iv) Ensure the hair is also firmly attached.

Say the words :

" be true "

(v) Send thoughts of love to your loved one and then snuff out the candles to "ground" the spell.

Everywhere your loved one goes, your
energy will go too, and their intentions
will be "buttoned-down" and not
inclined to wander.

NESTING INSTINCT!

Sometimes when you look into each other's eyes, the rest of the world just melts away.

If you wish it would melt away more often this spell will help you to stop a myriad of distractions from intruding.

DIFFICULTY	TIME TAKEN	RELIABILITY
♥ ♥	♥	♥ ♥ ♥

♡ YOU WILL NEED ♡

a small charm or trinket

belonging to each of you ~

a button, coin, or earring?

needle and thread (preferably silk)

handful of wool

or cotton ~

small piece of blue fabric   (to represent nesting material)

METHOD

(i) Carefully wrap the charms together in the cotton or wool so that they represent you and your lover snuggled together in a cozy nest.

(ii) Wrap the wool in the fabric and stitch it to form a small sealed parcel.

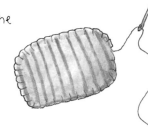

When you want some time and
space, take the little package and
place it by your door. You'll be
left alone to "nest-build" in peace.

SEALED WITH A KISS

If you're looking for commitment but your partner doesn't seem to have noticed (!) perform this spell and wait.

If, after one month, things have not become MUCH MORE SERIOUS, perhaps it's time to move on.

DIFFICULTY	TIME TAKEN	RELIABILITY
♥ ♥	♥ ♥	♥ ♥ ♥

♡ YOU WILL NEED ♡

Sheet of 100% linen paper
(art shops and good stationery
stock this)

cherry red lipstick

pin — represents the bond of love

cherry pit for a fruitful future

 (i) Put the lipstick on and plant a beautiful big red kiss on the paper!

(ii) Wrap the paper around the cherry pit and secure it with the pin.

(iii) Sneak round to your lover's place and "plant" it in their garden.

gardening gloves

flashlight

trowel

You have set the scene for love to blossom. Hopefully it will — if not, you know what they say:

he wasn't worth it anyway.

Sizzling cauldron

chapter

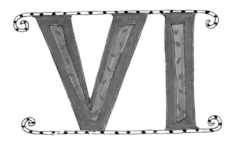

Hot stuff!

RECIPE FOR AN ANCIENT LOVE POTION

NOTE

This potion is reputed to have very powerful effects: YOU HAVE BEEN WARNED !!!

DIFFICULTY	TIME TAKEN	RELIABILITY
♥	♥	♥ ♥ ♥

♡ YOU WILL NEED ♡

some good robust red wine

plus:

a pinch of dried ginger
(for passion)

a dried chili pepper
(hot, hot, hot!)

large spoonful of honey

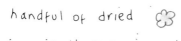

handful of dried
jasmine flowers   dash of vodka

METHOD

(i) Pour a generous slug of red wine into a pan over a low heat.

(ii) Add the ginger, honey, and a dash of vodka.

(iii) Place the chili pepper in the bottom of a wine glass and pour the potion onto it.

(iv) Float the jasmine flowers on the liquid.

This powerful potion should be drunk by you and your lover from the same glass.

(telephone off the hook!)

FLAME OF VENUS

Sometimes the sparkle seems to be missing from even the most perfect relationship. This lovely spell is performed by both of you to confirm your commitment and celebrate your love.

Venus the goddess of love will help to rekindle the embers.

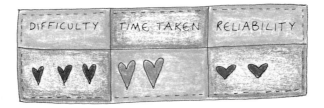

fresh rose petals

a small gift for each other

red candle

wooden bowl

pin - or tool for engraving the candle

NOTE Set the scene carefully; play beautiful music, dim the lights, prepare a special meal — at the very least, ban all telephones!

METHOD

(i) Each, in turn, engrave the other's initials along the candle and then light it.

(ii) Place each gift in the bowl and cover with rose petals.

(iii) Declare your love, in words, with a simple kiss ~ it's up to you.

(iv) Exchange gifts and snuff out the candle to ground the spell.

(v) Thank the goddess Venus for bringing you together...

You may
want to
save the
petals ~
scattering
them in a
special place
or keeping
them as
a talisman.

Treasure each gift and perform this
spell at intervals to keep the flame
eternally bright.

THE GARDEN OF LOVE

Romance will not flourish on barren ground. This spell will enable your own "garden of love" to blossom.

DIFFICULTY	TIME TAKEN	RELIABILITY
♥	♥ ♥ ♥	♥

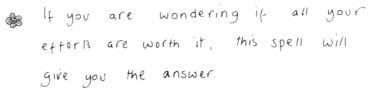

If you are wondering if all your efforts are worth it, this spell will give you the answer.

pomegranate

tomato
(or "love apple")

teaspoon of black peppercorns

ceramic pot

compost

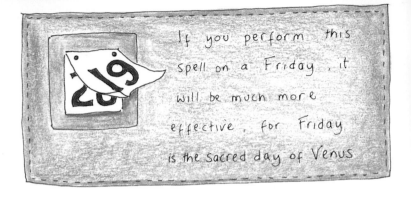

If you perform this spell on a Friday, it will be much more effective, for Friday is the sacred day of Venus

METHOD

(i) On a bright moonlit night, sit quietly and eat the pomegranate while you think of your loved one. Keep the seeds.

(ii) Do the same with the tomato.

(iii) Take all of the seeds and dry them.

(iv) Plant these, along with the peppercorns, in your pot and water regularly.

If a tiny fresh green leaf appears ~ all is well. If the earth remains bare ~ take up full time gardening instead.

new moon...

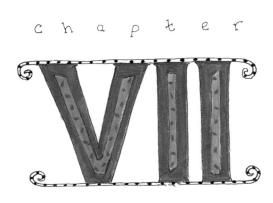

c h a p t e r

VII

Emergency spells~ first aid for romantics!

LUCKY IN LOVE

If you want to make a special date go "with a swing".

♡   YOU WILL NEED   ♡

thirteen red candles (!)

three drops of orange essential oil

three drops of patchouli essential oil

rose quartz crystal   marigold

METHOD

(i) Pluck the petals from the marigold and place in a bowl.

(ii) Add the essential oils.

(iii) Place the candles in a line and "anoint" each with the mixture, then light them.

(iv) Anoint the crystal. Snuff out the candles.

When you leave for your date, slip the crystal into your pocket and your beau will be putty in your hands!

 **BIG** love charm!

Make a bold statement of your love by hanging a talisman from a nearby tree that he (she) can't fail to notice. If he doesn't get the message— GIVE UP.

The first thing to do is make a large red heart— perhaps from a card or wood.

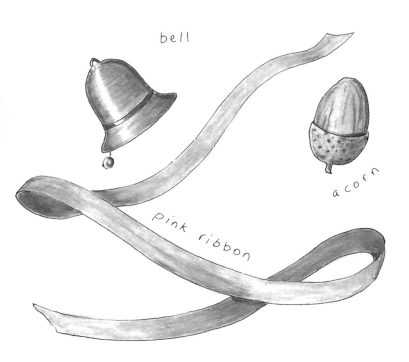

bell

acorn

pink ribbon

METHOD

(i) Wrap the ribbon around the acorn.

☆ Make sure you leave long ends on the ribbon.

(ii) Attach the bell and the heart.

(iii) Hang this from a high place so that its message can be carried by the wind.

When the breeze catches the bell, it will ring out your declaration of love.

If you are truly in love, the wind will carry this message to your lover and you will soon find out if he feels the same way.

QUEEN OF HEARTS

If you and your lover are parted and miss each other desperately ∿ this spell can ease the pain.

♡   YOU WILL NEED   ♡

The Queen of Hearts from a pack of playing cards

blue thread – preferably silk

nutmeg and grater

pink envelope

This spell has the advantage of being able to benefit each of you in turn, so it is performed in two parts.

★ Before you and your lover part,
take a length of thread and wear
it around your throat (see "note.")

blue thread necklace

Ask your lover to do the same and
then exchange lengths of thread.

NOTE

The throat is the center of power
in the body and so will transfer
your energy very effectively to
the "necklace."

 METHOD

(i) Take the queen of hearts playing card and tie the thread around it.

(ii) Place it in the envelope with a sprinkling of nutmeg. Seal the envelope with a kiss.

 It is very important that these are the only items in the envelope.

(iii) Place the envelope underneath your
pillow and while you sleep, you
will be united with your lover
in happy and vivid dreams.

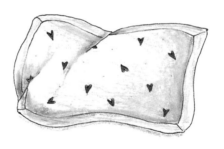

(iv) Untie the thread, and exchange it
for "your" piece of thread and reseal
the envelope.

(v) Send the envelope to your lover, so that they may share your dreams.

LOVE CAKES

Cakes are a symbol of love and generosity but they can also test your lover's fidelity!

YOU WILL NEED

The ingredients for making sponge cake

PLUS

some raisins and some fresh grapes

METHOD (i) Bake individual cupcakes placing a raisin in half of them, a grape in the other half.

♡ Do this by placing the fruit in the cupcake cup before adding the mixture

(iii) Offer the plate of cakes to your lover. If they choose a grape cake ~ fine. If they choose a raisin cake, their love is drying up and needs nurturing!

♡ The only consolation for this discovery is that you can eat all of the remaining cakes yourself!

OOPS!

Lovers' tiffs can leave scars. If you're still not talking but wish you were, this could break the silence!

♡ YOU WILL NEED ♡

a dove's feather — for peace and reconciliation

a lock of your hair

white candle — for purity

METHOD (i) Light the candle and meditate on your feelings of true regret.

(ii) Bind a few strands of your hair around the feather.

(iii) Secretly place this near your lover's car or bike.

antenna.   handlebar   gate post

Now when you contact your lover, your call will be welcomed and you will have proved your sincerity!

IT'S RAINING MEN !!!

The incredible success rate of the spells in this book may mean that you are faced with the problem of choosing between two (or more!) partners. To solve the big dilemma, conduct this quick and simple spell.

YOU WILL NEED

a small possession belonging to each partner: coin, cufflink, button, etc.

METHOD

(i) Stand outside in the light of a full bright moon.

(ii) Hold the items lightly in your left hand and say the words:

My true love will come to me and fulfill my destiny.

(iii) Toss the items high into the air and catch ONE.

He whose possession you hold in your hand is the one who is meant for you.

About the Author

"Adding a sprinkling of magic to the everyday" perfectly describes Lauren's original style of drawing. This is precisely what she does in her little books of spells.

Lauren lives in the Bedfordshire village of Cranfield where her family has lived for generations, although she studied fine art in Hull and London and worked as a wildlife illustrator before returning to the village. She shares what she describes as her "crumbling cottage" with her partner, Michael, and her "familiar," a little black dog called Jack. This is where she brews up her own spells and potions (of the gentlest kind), plays the piano, and stops the garden from invading the house!

Lauren loves drawing and always has a sketchbook in her pocket. In addition to her books of spells, Lauren has produced a series of six little gift books celebrating the simple things in life for MQ Publications, and her designs for Hotchpotch greeting cards are sold around the world.

First published by MQ Publications Limited
254-258 Goswell Road, London EC1V 7RL

Copyright © MQ Publications Limited 2000
Text and illustrations © Lauren White 2000

ISBN: 0-7407-0551-2

Library of Congress Catalog Card Number: 99-67080

1 3 5 7 9 0 8 6 4 2

Printed and bound in Italy